MESSY GOES TO OKIDO

The magic raindrops

Hello, I'm Messy. What's your name?

My name is

....

Thames & Hudson

Let's go to OKIDO!

Are you looking for adventure?
Is there something you need to know?
Come on, let's go to OKIDO!

Messy Monster

Zoe

Felix

Messy's best friends

Fluff

A friendly cloud

Find Foxy

Where is Foxy hiding in the story?

A clue – look somewhere hot and dry.

Zoom

A morphing master

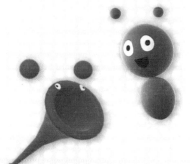

Mayor Oki

Mayor of OKIDO City

Zim

A super scientist

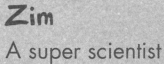

Zam

A great inventor

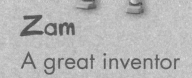

One hot, sunny day, Messy found Zoe and Felix sitting in the shade. They were waiting for Mayor Oki to judge their flowers in the City In Bloom competition.

Would you like to see our sunflowers, Messy?

Yes, please!

But the sunflowers didn't look very happy.
They were all **floppy** and **droopy**.

Zam's flowers were droopy too. She explained that plants need sunlight, air and water. The flowers in OKIDO were *floppy* because they were **thirsty**!

We have to save them before the competition!

Where can we get water from?

The three friends travelled to the desert to find the OKIDO tap.

Zoe and Felix pumped the handle **up and down**, but not a drop of water came out of the tap.

The pipe led to a river, but it was nearly dry. Zoe called Zim on her communicator.

Hi Zim, why can't we find any water?

It hasn't rained for days, and it won't rain any time soon. The sky is clear. Head for the mountains to find some clouds.

The gang jumped in Okidoodle and zoomed to the top of Rocky Mountain. A friendly white cloud appeared. Her name was Fluff.

Fluff got ready to rain. She collected tiny droplets of water from the air. The droplets were too **small** to see, but as Fluff filled up she grew **bigger** and **darker**.

Heeee-huh

Heeee-huh

Heeee-huh

Now I'm ready to rain!

There was no wind to **blow** Fluff to OKIDO City, so Felix attached a special sucker to the end of a rope.

Quack, quack!

Okidoodle pulled Fluff along. Fluff showered down rain.

Mayor Oki was about to start judging the flowers in the City In Bloom competition. As Fluff passed by, the floppy flowers sprang back to life – just like **magic**!

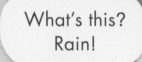

What's this? Rain!

When Fluff arrived at Felix's and Zoe's garden, she had just enough magic rain left to soak the **thirsty** sunflowers.

Fluff saved our sunflowers!

Look, here comes the mayor!

Mayor Oki thought the sunflowers looked wonderful.

Pah-pa-ra!

I declare Zoe and Felix the winners!

Hooray!

Fluff had done her job.
It was time for her to **float**
home to Rocky Mountain.

How is rain made?

Rain is made in a cloud high up in the sky. A cloud is full of tiny **droplets** of water that float up from Earth on a sunny day.

What happens up in the sky?

The tiny droplets of water join together to make a fluffy **cloud**.

Why does it rain?

When a cloud gets too heavy, it **rains**.

Zam's workshop

Turn water into tiny droplets.

Fill a cup with water and mark where the water reaches. Leave the cup in the sun.

Check the cup after a few hours. Some of the water has vanished into the air!

Giggle with the gang!

What does a cloud wear?

Thunderwear!

What happens when it rains cats and dogs?

Ha! Ha!

You step in a poodle!

First published in the United Kingdom in 2015 by Thames & Hudson Ltd, 181A High Holborn, London WC1V 7QX

Licensed by Doodle Productions Limited based on the TV series 'Messy Goes to OKIDO'

The magic raindrops © 2015 Thames & Hudson Ltd, London

OKIDO content and logo © 2015 Doodle Productions Limited

OKIDO and MESSY and are trademarks of Doodle Productions Limited

Printed and bound in China by Toppan Leefung Printing Limited

British Library Cataloguing-in-Publication Data
A catalogue record for this book is available from the British Library

ISBN 978-0-500-65063-9

To find out about all our publications, please visit **www.thamesandhudson.com**. There you can subscribe to our e-newsletter, browse or download our current catalogue, and buy any titles that are in print.